Are you ready to be a leader?

The Essential Steps to Becoming a Leader

OrangeBooks Publication

1st Floor, Rajhans Arcade, Mall Road, Kohka, Bhilai, Chhattisgarh 490020

Website: **www.orangebooks.in**

© Copyright, 2024, Author

All rights reserved. No part of this book may be reproduced, stored in a retrieval system, or transmitted, in any form by any means, electronic, mechanical, magnetic, optical, chemical, manual, photocopying, recording or otherwise, without the prior written consent of its writer.

First Edition, 2024

ISBN: 978-93-5621-762-1

ARE YOU *Ready* TO BE A LEADER?

THE ESSENTIAL STEPS TO BECOMING A LEADER

MAKI ISMAIL

OrangeBooks Publication
www.orangebooks.in

Contents

- Introduction 1
- The Journey of Leadership 6
- Step 1: Understanding Your Own Strengths and Weaknesses as a Leader 24
- Step 2: Mastering the Art of Communication 39
- Step 3: Developing Strategies to effectively Manage Change & Conflict 52
- Step 4: Building Relationships with Team Members & Stakeholders 69
- Conclusion 81

Introduction

Stepping into Leadership

Have you ever wondered what makes a leader? Not just any leader, but a truly effective one who sparks change and stirs enthusiasm? Leadership is not confined to boardrooms or battlefields; it is a vital pulse in every corner of life, from bustling offices to quiet neighborhood gatherings and lively family dinners. This book is your gateway to understanding that leadership is much more than a title—it is an adventure in influencing and uplifting others.

The Art of Leadership

What does it take to be a leader? This is not just about the authority or the ability to command; it is about the art of steering a diverse group of people towards a shared dream. Leadership permeates every aspect of life: from the corporate executives strategizing in high-stakes boardrooms to community leaders orchestrating local initiatives, and even within the dynamics of a family setting. This book will guide you through the multifaceted landscape of leadership, revealing that true leadership is not merely a role but a profound journey of influence and inspiration.

The Essence of True Leadership

Think of leadership as a craft, one that blends intuition with strategy, empathy with decisiveness. It involves:

- **Masterful Communication:** A leader articulates visions so compellingly that others can't help but follow.

- **Deep Empathy:** Understanding the beats of your team's hearts, foreseeing their needs, and standing in their shoes.

- **Unwavering Integrity:** Being the moral compass that remains true even when storms hit.

- **Inspirational Drive:** Fueling the fire of passion and perseverance that keeps the team striving forward, especially when the odds are stacked against them.

- **Creative Vision:** Pioneering innovative paths and embracing unconventional ideas that break boundaries and set new standards.

The Tale of Alex: A Natural Leader

Once upon a time, in a small village, there was a group of friends who loved playing football. They would gather every evening at a local field and play their hearts out. Among them, there was a young boy named Alex who possessed natural leadership qualities. He had the special talent to bring people together, to make them act together to achieve a common goal. Every time they played, Alex would take charge, organize the teams, and motivate everyone to give their best. His enthusiasm and ability to inspire others made him a natural leader on the field. As time went on, the village decided to organize a football tournament with neighbouring communities. They needed someone to lead the team, and naturally, they turned to Alex. He gladly accepted the responsibility and immediately set to work. He gathered the team, discussed strategies, and set goals for everyone to strive towards. He conveyed a strong sense of direction, emphasizing the importance of teamwork and dedication. With Alex as their leader, the team practiced tirelessly, honing their skills and building camaraderie. Their hard work paid off as they performed exceptionally well in the tournament. They not only won the tournament but also earned the respect and admiration of their opponents. Being a leader means having the ability to bring people together, motivate them, and guide them towards a common goal.

Now let us dive into the story of Alex and learn from it, a young, charismatic leader whose influence began on the football field of his small village. Alex did not just play; he transformed each game into a lesson in leadership. When a regional tournament arose, Alex was the unanimous choice to lead. His leadership was magnetic, pulling his teammates into a circle of shared purpose. They were no longer just players; they became part of a movement, a narrative of unity and effort that Alex orchestrated with natural flair. Their eventual victory at the tournament was a testament to how effective leadership can elevate ordinary efforts into extraordinary achievements.

Leadership for the Future

In our ever-evolving world, where digital revolutions and cultural shifts redefine the old norms, leadership too must evolve. This book does not just stick to traditional views but expands into how modern dynamics shift the leadership landscape. You will explore how today's leaders navigate through technological advancements, global interconnectedness, and cultural diversity. We will discuss tools and techniques that modern leaders use to stay ahead, ensuring their leadership is not only effective but also inclusive and forward-thinking.

Embarking on Your Leadership Journey

Each person's journey to leadership is distinct—a path laden with unique challenges and milestones. This book will serve as your compass, offering you a myriad of insights, from understanding the psychological underpinnings of leadership to practical tips for daily leadership living. We will delve into stories of renowned leaders who have shaped the world, drawing lessons from their experiences.

Your path to leadership is unique and full of potential. As we explore the essence of inspiring, guiding, and molding the future, you will discover practical steps and transformative insights to foster your leadership qualities. Each chapter is a stepping-stone to becoming a leader who does not just exist but significantly impacts the world.

Get ready to engage deeply with your own leadership potential, to refine your skills and broaden your understanding. Each chapter will build on the last, forming a comprehensive guide designed to unlock your potential as a leader who not only leads but also inspires, innovates, and transforms.

Prepare to embark on an enlightening journey, to not just learn about leadership but to live it. By turning these pages, you step closer to becoming the leader who not only directs but dynamically enhances the lives of those they lead, leaving a legacy of positive impact and transformative power.

Get ready to turn the pages of your leadership story, filled with insights, challenges, and triumphs. Together, we will unlock the leader within you, ready to make a lasting imprint on the world around you.

Chapter 1

The Journey of Leadership

Leadership is more than a role; it is an epic journey of transformation and unity. Picture it as a voyage across vast oceans, where each wave represents a challenge to overcome and each calm stretch a moment to reflect and grow. This journey is not just about reaching a destination but about evolving with every experience, learning from each trial, and inspiring those around you to rise together.

Imagine you are steering a ship through both calm and stormy seas. As a leader, you need to be brave, ready to face the unknown, and flexible enough to handle changes and challenges. Leadership is your journey through new experiences, where you learn how to make a real difference.

Leadership is a challenging and complex journey that requires constant adaptation, resilience, and perseverance. Leadership is not a destination, but a continuous journey of growth and learning. Leaders must navigate through uncharted territory, facing both successes and failures, while having the courage to make tough decisions.

Imagine embarking on an epic journey—one not marked by maps or milestones, but by growth, challenges, and the relentless pursuit of greatness. Leadership is that odyssey. It's not a static state but an evolving expedition that demands courage, adaptability, and an unwavering commitment to forge ahead despite daunting challenges. This chapter unfolds the rich tapestry of leadership—a narrative woven from trials, triumphs, and the unyielding spirit of those who dare to lead.

Embarking on the Uncharted

Imagine setting sail into unknown waters—this is the essence of leadership. It requires the courage to navigate through uncertainty and the resilience to weather storms. Leaders are pioneers, charting courses not just for themselves but also for whole communities. Each decision shapes the journey, not just directing the path but also defining the leader's legacy.

The journey of leadership is filled with challenges, obstacles, and constant changes that require adaptability and resilience. Leaders must be willing to take risks, make bold moves, and navigate unexplored paths. They must also have the courage to make difficult decisions and manage both success and failure.

The journey of leadership demands constant self-reflection, learning, and adaptation. It is a path that is often marked by setbacks and failures, but true leaders rise above them, gaining wisdom and resilience along the way.

Leadership is often forged through a complex interplay of experiences, challenges, and personal growth. Exploring the stories of individuals who have risen to leadership positions reveals a wealth of insight into the qualities and traits that define exceptional leaders.

Overcoming Adversity

Through the annals of history, leaders have often been forged in the crucibles of hardship. Each challenge they overcome, each barrier they break, adds to their resilience and fortitude. The tales of such leaders are not merely stories; they are lessons in the art of perseverance—testaments to the human spirit's capacity to transcend limitations.

True leaders are often sculpted by the trials they face. Like seasoned sailors who learn to read the wind and waves, leaders grow stronger with each challenge. Many leaders have faced significant adversity on their path to leadership. From overcoming personal hardships to navigating professional setbacks, these experiences have shaped their resilience and determination. In this chapter, we are going to dive into stories of those who faced formidable obstacles yet emerged not only unbroken but also empowered. Their resilience teaches us that the true measure of a leader is not how they triumph but how they transcend difficulties.

By delving into their stories, we gain a deeper understanding of the perseverance and fortitude required to lead effectively.

Vision and Inspiration

Great leaders are visionaries. They have the unique ability to inspire others with groundbreaking ideas, compelling communication, and an unyielding pursuit of excellence. Their stories illuminate the transformative power of a clear vision and the capacity to motivate others towards achieving a shared goal.

What sets a true leader apart is the clarity of their vision and their unwavering commitment to achieve it. Great leaders have clear visions—they see what others don't. They can guide people towards exciting new goals. Here, we'll learn about the lives of visionary leaders who have inspired revolutions, led movements, and changed the course of history. From Nelson Mandela's unshakeable resolve to unify a nation to Mahatma Gandhi's staunch advocacy for nonviolence—these leaders exemplified how a single compelling vision can mobilize masses and forge new destinies.

Imagine a leader whose vision ignites the flames of change, whose words inspire action and whose dreams reshape realities. Those are leaders like Nelson Mandela and Mahatma Gandhi, who had strong beliefs and led people to make huge changes. Their stories show how having a strong, clear vision can motivate everyone to work together and achieve great things.

Effective leaders are often driven by a powerful vision and a desire to inspire others. Whether through innovative ideas, compelling communication, or a relentless pursuit of excellence, these individuals have the ability to ignite passion and motivation in those around them. Exploring their journeys sheds light on the transformative impact of a clear vision and the ability to inspire others towards a common goal.

Building Empathy and Connection

Leadership transcends the mechanics of management—it is about connecting hearts and minds. Leadership is as much about connecting with people, understanding needs, respecting perspectives, and building bridges as it is about setting strategic direction. By examining the experiences of leaders who have demonstrated remarkable empathy and a genuine connection with others, we uncover the critical importance of understanding and valuing individual perspectives. Their stories provide valuable lessons in building meaningful relationships and fostering a culture of inclusivity and collaboration.

As we delve into these stories of leadership, we uncover the multifaceted nature of leadership development and the myriad pathways through which individuals emerge as impactful leaders. By embracing the depth of these narratives, we gain invaluable insights that can illuminate our own journey towards leadership.

Let's embark on an enlightening journey through the stories of distinguished leaders from diverse backgrounds. As we navigate their unique paths to success, you will gain a richer, more nuanced understanding of the essence of true leadership. We will extract pivotal lessons and practical strategies from their experiences—tools that you can integrate into your own approach to leadership. This exploration is designed not just to inform but also to transform, equipping you with the knowledge and skills necessary to inspire, motivate, and lead with confidence and effectiveness.

Join me as we uncover the keys to unlocking your full potential as a dynamic leader in today's world.

Nelson Mandela: A Legacy of Reconciliation

Nelson Mandela's life journey is not just a narrative of personal triumph but a testament to the profound impact of transformational leadership on society. His story unfolds in the crucible of apartheid—a systematic and brutal regime of racial segregation in South Africa that oppressed the majority black population while privileging a white minority.

Early Life and Political Awakening

Born in 1918 in the village of Mvezo, in what is now Eastern Cape, Mandela was initially named Rolihlahla, which colloquially translates to "troublemaker." His father's death when Mandela was nine years old marked a pivotal turn, leading to his guardianship under Jongintaba Dalindyebo, the acting regent of the Thembu people. This period in Mandela's life was critical in shaping his understanding of leadership and governance, as he was exposed to the operations of tribal leadership, which subtly laid the groundwork for his later political engagement.

The Spear of the Nation

Mandela's transformation into a revolutionary leader began at the University of Fort Hare and continued in Johannesburg, where he pursued legal studies and encountered the stark realities of racial discrimination. Joining the African National Congress (ANC) in 1943, he was instrumental in founding the ANC Youth League. Mandela's leadership took on a more radical trajectory with the launch of the armed wing of the ANC, Umkhonto we Sizwe, in 1961, reflecting his belief that non-violent protest alone could not achieve the end of apartheid.

The Prison Years: A Crucible of Leadership

Mandela's 27 years in prison, beginning in 1962, were transformative. Incarcerated in Robben Island, Pollsmoor, and Victor Verster prisons, he faced harsh conditions that tested and ultimately honed his resolve and leadership skills. During this time, Mandela's ideology evolved from militant freedom fighter to a sage advocate of reconciliation and negotiation, embodying the philosophy that his personal suffering was a microcosm of the broader struggle against oppression.

Pathway to Peace and Reconciliation

Released in 1990 amid escalating domestic and international pressure, Mandela's emergence as a free man was symbolic of the potential for a new South Africa. His negotiations with the apartheid government and then-President F.W. de Klerk paved the way for the 1994 democratic elections, where Mandela was elected as South Africa's first black president. His presidency was marked by the establishment of the Truth and Reconciliation Commission, aimed at healing the wounds of apartheid by uncovering the truth about past abuses and fostering a new era of understanding.

Legacy and Global Influence

Mandela's legacy transcends the borders of South Africa, symbolizing global aspirations for freedom and equality. He remained a stalwart champion for peace, democracy, and social justice until his death in 2013. His ability to forgive his oppressors and to channel his years of struggle into policies that built a nation are what make his journey truly transformational.

Nelson Mandela's life reminds us that leadership is not about power, but about empowering others. It is a lesson in resilience, moral integrity, and the indomitable power of human spirit to overcome adversity. His story continues to inspire leaders and individuals around the world to fight for justice and equality in their own communities and nations.

To summarize, Nelson Mandela's journey from a young anti-apartheid activist to becoming the first black President of South Africa is a testament to the transformative power of resilience, courage, and leadership. Born into the Thembu royal family, Mandela initially pursued a career in law, only to be drawn into the political struggle against the oppressive apartheid regime. His unwavering commitment to justice and equality led to his imprisonment for 27 years. However, Mandela's spirit remained unbroken, and upon his release, he dedicated himself to unifying a divided nation and steering it towards reconciliation and democracy. Mandela's exemplary leadership and ability to forgive his oppressors have made him a revered global symbol of peace and justice.

Mahatma Gandhi: The Architect of Nonviolence

Mahatma Gandhi, often revered as the 'Father of the Nation' in India, exemplified visionary leadership that transcended geopolitical boundaries and left an indelible mark on global peace movements. His philosophy of nonviolent resistance, or **Satyagraha**, redefined the approach to civil disobedience and political activism, influencing leaders and social movements worldwide.

Early Influences and Philosophical Foundations

Born in 1869 in Porbandar, India, Mohandas Karamchand Gandhi was influenced early by the Jain religious tenets of nonviolence and vegetarianism prevalent in his home state of Gujarat. His time in London and later in South Africa was pivotal, exposing him to racial discrimination and social injustice, shaping his socio-political activism. It was in South Africa where Gandhi first applied his theory of nonviolent resistance, advocating for the rights of the Indian minority.

Satyagraha: The Pillar of Nonviolent Resistance

Gandhi introduced **Satyagraha** in India's struggle for independence from British rule. This method of nonviolent resistance involved peaceful protests, non-cooperation, and other forms of civil disobedience. This approach not only mobilized masses in India from diverse socio-economic backgrounds but also highlighted the moral high ground of the Indian independence movement against the often brutal tactics of the British colonial forces.

Salt March: A Defining Moment

The 1930 Salt March was a prime example of Gandhi's visionary leadership. In protest against the British salt tax, a critical and oppressive economic measure affecting the common populace, Gandhi led thousands on a 240-mile march to the Arabian Sea to make their own salt. This act of defiance not only galvanized Indian sentiment against British rule but also captured the world's attention, demonstrating the power of collective action and moral resistance.

Influence Beyond Borders

Gandhi's impact was not confined to India. His principles influenced global icons such as Martin Luther King Jr. in the United States, Nelson Mandela in South Africa, and many other civil rights leaders from various countries. Through his actions and teachings, Gandhi demonstrated that steadfast adherence to nonviolence could dismantle oppressive structures without recourse to violence.

Challenges and Critiques

Despite his visionary leadership, Gandhi faced criticism, including his stringent practices of fasting and his unorthodox views on diet and medicine. Some contemporaries and later scholars have critiqued his approaches as impractical or overly idealistic in certain political contexts. Moreover, his role in partition and his efforts to reconcile Hindu-Muslim relations in a rapidly polarizing India mark complex aspects of his leadership.

Legacy and Continuing Relevance

Gandhi's vision for an independent India based on religious pluralism, nonviolence, and socio-economic justice remains relevant. His commitment to simplicity, ethical governance, and the empowerment of the marginalized continues to inspire and challenge current and future leaders.

Mahatma Gandhi's legacy teaches us that true leadership is rooted in the courage to uphold one's principles in the face of adversity and the ability to inspire and mobilize others towards a common, noble cause. His life remains a testament to the enduring power of nonviolent resistance and the impact of visionary leadership on societal change.

To conclude, Mahatma Gandhi, fondly known as the "Father of the Nation" in India, is celebrated for his visionary leadership in the pursuit of Indian independence from British colonial rule. Gandhi's philosophy of nonviolent resistance, known as Satyagraha, inspired millions to join the freedom struggle. His unwavering resolve, based on principles of truth and nonviolence, not only mobilized the masses but also influenced movements for civil rights and freedom across the globe. Through his selfless dedication and moral authority, Gandhi's leadership transcended borders and continues to be a guiding light for leaders advocating peaceful resistance and social change.

Malala Yousafzai: The Voice of Courage

Malala Yousafzai's story is a profound testament to resilience, courage, and the relentless pursuit of education under extraordinarily oppressive conditions. Her journey from a young schoolgirl in Pakistan's Swat Valley to a global advocate for girls' education encapsulates her indomitable spirit and unyielding dedication to human rights.

Early Life and Advocacy

Born in 1997 in Mingora, Swat Valley, a region then under the oppressive control of the Tehrik-i-Taliban Pakistan (TTP), Malala was raised in an environment where education for girls was systematically dismantled by extremist forces. Despite these challenges, Malala's father, Ziauddin Yousafzai, an educator himself, instilled in her a passion for learning and a belief in the power of education. From a young age, Malala began advocating for girls' education, which was directly contrary to the Taliban's edicts.

Targeted for Her Beliefs

Malala's advocacy did not go unnoticed. In 2012, at the age of 15, she was brutally attacked by a Taliban gunman who boarded her school bus and shot her in the head. The attack was intended to silence her and, by extension, any similar efforts advocating for girls' education. However, it had the opposite effect, galvanizing the global community and bringing international attention to the issue of educational rights in regions under Taliban influence.

Recovery and Continued Advocacy

Miraculously surviving the attack, Malala's recovery in the United Kingdom became a turning point in her life. As she regained her strength, her resolve to continue her mission only deepened. Malala took her campaign to a global stage, addressing the United Nations on her 16th birthday, which was later declared "Malala Day" in her honor. Her speech passionately reiterated her commitment to education and women's rights, highlighting her resilience and determination to not let the attack define her limitations.

Nobel Peace Prize and Beyond

In 2014, Malala was co-recipient of the Nobel Peace Prize, becoming the youngest-ever laureate, recognized for her struggle against the suppression of children and young people and for the right of all children to education. The Malala Fund, co-founded with her father, is another beacon of her commitment, focusing on advocacy, funding, and creating awareness for girls' education worldwide.

Impact and Legacy

Malala's resilience has not only changed the landscape for educational advocacy but also inspired a generation of girls and young women to demand their right to education. Her story is a reminder of the oppressive conditions many girls still endure in their pursuit of an education. Through her public appearances, writings, and the work of her fund, Malala continues to be a leading voice in advocating for educational policies that ensure free, safe, and quality schooling for every girl around the world.

In summary, Malala Yousafzai's life journey underscores that resilience can transform personal tragedy into a global dialogue for change. Her courage, conviction, and relentless pursuit of her goals remind us that one young person's voice can, indeed, echo across the globe, initiating widespread social and political change.

To conclude, Malala Yousafzai, a Pakistani education activist, gained global recognition for her unwavering courage and advocacy for girls' education, even in the face of grave danger. At the tender age of 15, Malala survived an assassination attempt by the Taliban, a testament to her unyielding commitment to standing up against injustice. Despite the harrowing experience, Malala persevered and became a powerful voice for education and women's rights worldwide, ultimately becoming the youngest-ever Nobel Prize laureate. Her remarkable resilience and determination in the face of adversity serve as an inspiration for leaders and advocates striving to create a more equitable and inclusive world.

Amina: The Heart of the Community

Once upon a time, in a small village nestled in the heart of the mountains, there lived a wise and compassionate leader named Amina. She was known for her ability to listen to her people and make decisions that were in the best interest of the entire community. She was a source of guidance and support for everyone around her, and her leadership style inspired others to do their best.

Amina believed that being a leader meant not only making decisions, but also empowering others to become leaders in their own right. She encouraged open communication and collaboration, creating an environment where everyone's opinions were valued. Amina's commitment to serving her community and leading with integrity made her a role model for all who knew her.

One day, a great storm hit the village, causing widespread damage to homes and crops. Amina immediately sprang into action, organizing relief efforts and ensuring that everyone had the support they needed to rebuild. Her selfless dedication to her people during this crisis further solidified her reputation as a true leader.

As the village recovered and flourished once again, Amina's legacy continued to inspire future generations to lead with compassion, empathy, and a strong sense of community. Amina's story serves as a timeless reminder of what it truly means to be a leader.

Being a leader means having the ability to listen, make decisions in the best interest of the community, empower others to become leaders, serve with integrity, and inspire others through compassionate and selfless actions.

David's Story: The Compassionate Warrior

There was a young man named David who lived in a small village. David was known for his kindness, compassion, and ability to bring people together. As he grew older, David took on more responsibilities in the village, helping to resolve disputes, organizing community events, and offering a listening ear to those in need. His natural ability to lead and inspire others became evident to everyone around him.

People looked up to David and sought his guidance in times of trouble. He never turned anyone away and always made time to lend a helping hand. Over time, David's reputation as a leader grew, and he found himself at the forefront of important decisions and initiatives within the village.

Despite his growing influence, David remained humble and focused on serving the best interests of the community. He believed that true leadership was not about exerting authority, but about empowering others and working together towards common goals. David's selfless dedication and unwavering integrity made him a role model for the entire village.

As the years passed, David's leadership extended beyond the village, impacting the surrounding regions and inspiring others to follow his example. His story became a timeless lesson in the true meaning of leadership – a journey marked by empathy, resilience, and a commitment to making a positive difference in the lives of others. Being a leader means having the ability to bring people together, inspire others, and selflessly serve the best interests of the community.

The Village Elder: Wisdom without a Throne

There was a humble city, where the people lived simple yet fulfilling lives. At the heart of the village was a wise elder who was revered by all for his leadership and guidance. He was always willing to listen to the concerns of the villagers and offer thoughtful advice. Despite not holding an official title, he was undoubtedly the leader of the community.

The elder demonstrated the true essence of leadership through his selflessness, empathy, and ability to unite the villagers during times of joy and sorrow. His actions inspired others to act with compassion and generosity, creating a harmonious and supportive environment for all.

As the years passed, the elder passed on his wisdom to the younger generation, instilling in them the values of integrity, responsibility, and empathy. These future leaders carried forward the legacy of their mentor, ensuring that the village continued to thrive under their guidance.

The story of the humble elder serves as a testament to the fact that authority or power does not define true leadership, but by the impact one has on others and the ability to bring out the best in those around them. Being a leader means embodying qualities such as selflessness, empathy, and the ability to unite and inspire others.

These exemplary stories of leadership offer profound insights into the transformative journeys of individuals who reshaped societies and inspired change through their vision, resilience, and unwavering commitment to justice and equality.

Join me on this journey as we seek to unravel the true essence of being a leader.

Step 1: Understanding Your Own Strengths and Weaknesses as a Leader

Introduction

Leadership is a journey that begins with a single, yet profound, step: understanding yourself. Imagine you are an experienced sailor setting out to navigate the vast oceans. Just as a sailor must understand the strengths and limitations of their vessel, a leader must grasp their own capabilities and weaknesses. This knowledge is not only crucial for steering through calm waters but imperative when storms arise. As a leader, understanding your own strengths and weaknesses is crucial for personal and professional growth. It is important to not only recognize your strengths but also leverage them to achieve success. Reflect on the skills and qualities that have helped you excel in leadership roles. Are you a great communicator, a strategic thinker, or a skilled problem-solver? These strengths can be your foundation for leading and inspiring others. By recognizing and leveraging your strengths, you lay the foundation for effective leadership.

On the other hand, acknowledging your weaknesses is equally important. Be honest with yourself about areas where you may need improvement. Do you struggle with delegating tasks, managing time effectively, or adapting to change? By identifying these weaknesses, you can actively work on developing new skills and seeking support where needed. Recognizing and addressing your weaknesses is a sign of self-awareness and a key step towards becoming a more effective leader. This recognition is not a sign of failure but a step toward becoming a more effective leader.

Regular reassessment of your strengths and weaknesses, coupled with feedback from peers and professional development opportunities, underpins continuous improvement. Remember, effective leadership is not about perfection but about constant growth and inspiring the same in others.

The Story of the Reflective Leader

Alex, a seasoned project manager, had always taken pride in his strategic acumen and exceptional communication abilities, attributes that had driven the success of numerous project launches under his leadership. However, despite these strengths, Alex grappled with one significant challenge: delegation. He often found himself overwhelmed, burdened by a workload that should have been distributed among his team.

One reflective day, after navigating through the complexities of a particularly demanding project, Alex realized the necessity of reassessing his approach. In a moment of introspection, he decided to solicit feedback from his team—a decision that proved transformative. The insights he received were not only eye-opening but also somewhat disconcerting; his team members felt underutilized and expressed a strong desire to contribute more meaningfully to projects.

This feedback served as a crucial wake-up call for Alex. Recognizing the untapped potential of his team and the inefficiencies of his current management style, he embarked on a mission to enhance his delegation skills. This shift in perspective marked the beginning of a significant transformation, not just for Alex but for his entire team.

Determined to turn this personal shortcoming into a growth opportunity, Alex started by setting clear expectations and defining roles more precisely for each team member. He took the time to understand the individual strengths and aspirations of his team, aligning tasks with their capabilities and career goals. This not only maximized efficiency but also fostered a sense of ownership and responsibility among the team members.

Through regular feedback sessions and open communication channels, Alex encouraged his team to voice their ideas and concerns, ensuring that delegation was not just a distribution of tasks but a collaborative and dynamic process. This new approach led to more engaged and motivated team members, who felt valued and acknowledged for their contributions.

As Alex refined his delegation techniques, he witnessed a remarkable change in the team dynamics and project outcomes. The projects under his leadership were not only completed more efficiently but also with a higher degree of innovation and creativity. Alex's ability to transform a personal weakness into a tool for team empowerment and growth not only enhanced his leadership capabilities but also drove his team toward unprecedented success.

1. Deepening Self-Awareness

Understanding your strengths and weaknesses involves deep introspection. It's not merely about recognizing what you excel at or fall short of, but understanding the underlying causes. By exploring these, you can develop targeted strategies for leveraging your strengths and improving weaknesses, thus enhancing your leadership effectiveness.

For instance, uncovering the roots of your strengths may reveal unique qualities that set you apart. Similarly, understanding why certain tasks are challenging can lead to specific improvements, making your approach to leadership more effective and authentic.

- **Deepening Self-Awareness through Story**

Consider Sarah, CEO of a thriving tech start-up, was a powerhouse of innovation. Her sharp problem-solving skills had catapulted her company ahead of the competition, but her relentless drive for speed was taking its toll on her team. They were burning out, and she was too caught up in her rapid pace to notice.

It was during a routine team meeting that everything came to light. A trusted colleague, someone who had been with Sarah from the start, took a deep breath and voiced the unspoken truth: the team was struggling. They were tired, stressed, and becoming increasingly disconnected from the mission they once pursued with passion. This intervention was a jolt for Sarah, piercing her bubble of relentless progress to reveal the weary faces of her team.

Stunned by this revelation, Sarah took a hard look at her leadership style. She realized that while she was pushing her team towards innovation, she was inadvertently pushing them towards exhaustion as well. Determined to change, she began holding regular feedback sessions, inviting her team to share their honest thoughts and feelings.

These sessions opened Sarah's eyes even further. Every conversation, every shared concern, every suggestion helped her see not just the mechanics of her business, but the human element she'd been overlooking. She learned about the long hours, the skipped lunches, the personal sacrifices her team was making to keep up with her pace.

Moved by their dedication and candid feedback, Sarah started to make real changes. She adjusted project timelines, set more realistic goals, and began recognizing and celebrating the team's hard work. More importantly, she started to prioritize their well-being, encouraging them to take time off and disconnect when needed.

This shift in her approach brought a new energy to the team. They started to feel valued not just for their output, but for their well-being. As Sarah adapted her leadership to nurture her team, they reconnected with their original passion for the startup's mission. Together, they moved forward, not just as a company, but as a united group of individuals driven by a common purpose, revitalized by a leader who truly saw and supported them.

Self-Assessment for Effective Leadership

Self-assessment is critical in leadership. It involves a detailed evaluation of your abilities, behaviors, and characteristics, requiring you to look beyond superficial qualities to how these traits manifest in real-world leadership situations. Engaging with feedback from others provides additional perspectives that enrich your understanding of your leadership style.

- **Self-Assessment as a Narrative of Growth through story**

Michael, the dedicated director of a non-profit, deeply understood that true leadership blossomed from self-awareness and continuous personal growth. Recognizing the complex demands of his role, he committed himself to regular periods of self-reflection, a practice that became a cornerstone of his leadership.

Each session was an opportunity for Michael to sit quietly, away from the hustle of daily operations, and dive into a thorough examination of his recent actions and decisions. He celebrated his successes, like the times his empathetic approach had rallied his team during tough fundraising campaigns, acknowledging how his ability to connect on a human level had been a key driver of their achievements.

However, Michael was equally focused on areas where he fell short. He often grappled with indecisiveness when faced with tough choices, a weakness that sometimes slowed the momentum of his team and blurred the clarity of their mission. He knew that every moment spent in hesitation was a missed opportunity to drive change.

These introspective sessions weren't easy, often filled with hard truths about the gaps between his intentions and his actions. Yet, Michael embraced this process with open arms, understanding that each insight gained was a stepping stone towards becoming a more effective leader.

Armed with this self-knowledge, Michael took proactive steps to mitigate his weaknesses. He sought advice from mentors, engaged in leadership workshops, and started making more deliberate decisions to build his confidence. His efforts paid off gradually, as he noticed a positive shift in how he led his team and made strategic decisions.

Michael's commitment to self-assessment did more than just foster his personal growth—it also steered his organization through numerous challenges. By continually adapting and evolving, he kept his team motivated and resilient, ready to navigate the ever-changing landscape of non-profit work. His story is a testament to the power of reflection in leadership, highlighting how a deep understanding of oneself can inspire growth and lead to greater achievements.

2. Identifying Personal Leadership Strengths

Recognizing personal leadership strengths goes beyond identifying obvious skills. It involves understanding how these strengths interconnect with your core values and impact your team's performance and well-being. Knowing how these strengths contribute to team motivation and engagement provides deeper insights into your effectiveness as a leader.

- **Identifying Personal Leadership Strengths through story**

Lisa, the principal of a bustling high school, was celebrated not just for her eloquence but for her profound ability to connect with her staff and students on a deeper level. Her communication skills went beyond mere clarity of speech; they were about opening doors to meaningful dialogue and creating a nurturing environment that everyone in the school benefitted from.

Each day, as she walked the hallways of her school, Lisa's approach was always the same: listen intently, respond thoughtfully, and ensure that everyone felt heard and valued. This ability to engage was not just a skill but a gift that Lisa had honed over the years, knowing that the heart of her school's success lay in the strength of its community.

When conflicts arose, as they inevitably do in any dynamic school environment, Lisa's talents truly shone. She had a unique way of transforming what could be contentious interactions into opportunities for growth and understanding. For instance, during staff meetings or student council sessions, she encouraged open communication, inviting opinions and concerns. Lisa listened not just to respond, but to understand, often paraphrasing what others had said to confirm her understanding and to show that every voice was important.

Her empathetic responses and willingness to consider diverse perspectives turned potential battlegrounds into forums for collaborative problem-solving. Teachers felt supported and valued, knowing their input had a direct impact on school policies and practices. Students, too, sensed that their opinions mattered, which empowered them and deepened their respect for the school administration.

Under Lisa's leadership, the high school thrived as a model of efficiency and harmony. Her knack for empathetic communication fostered an atmosphere where staff and students alike felt motivated and engaged, contributing to a positive, productive learning environment. Her legacy was not just in the academic success of her students but in the strong, compassionate community she built through her exceptional ability to connect and communicate.

3. Strategies for Leveraging Leadership Strengths

Developing strategies to maximize your strengths involves aligning them with leadership goals and seeking opportunities that highlight these strengths. Collaborating with others whose strengths complement yours can create powerful synergies, enhancing team performance and leadership impact.

- **Strategies for Leveraging Leadership Strengths through story**

James, a seasoned corporate leader, was well-known for his visionary thinking—a skill that allowed him to see beyond the immediate horizon and anticipate the future needs of the business. Recognizing this unique ability as his greatest asset, James strategically positioned himself to lead projects that were not only innovative but also critical to his company's growth.

Instead of fitting into traditional roles that might limit his creative potential, James actively sought opportunities where he could apply his forward-thinking skills. He became the driving force behind groundbreaking projects, such as the integration of AI technology in their customer service operations, which revolutionized how the company interacted with its clients.

By aligning his role with his strengths, James not only excelled personally but also significantly enhanced his team's performance. His projects consistently delivered impressive results, setting new benchmarks for innovation within the company. This success was not lost on his peers and the higher management, who began to see the immense value in leveraging individual strengths for organizational benefit.

James's approach also served as a vibrant example for his colleagues. He demonstrated that when employees are empowered to match their job roles with their personal strengths, they can achieve much more than in traditional, rigidly defined positions. This led to a cultural shift within the company, where other leaders started to encourage their team members to explore and exploit their unique skills, further fostering an environment of growth and innovation.

Under James's leadership, the company not only saw a surge in creativity and productivity but also became a magnet for top talent who were eager to work in a place that valued personal strengths and offered roles that could lead to remarkable achievements. His visionary approach proved to be a catalyst for change, inspiring an entire organization to evolve and thrive by aligning roles with the intrinsic strengths of its people.

4. Recognizing and Addressing Leadership Weaknesses

Acknowledging weaknesses is crucial for personal growth. Understanding these areas deeply, including their origins, helps formulate effective improvement strategies.

Embracing vulnerabilities and being open to feedback are signs of strong leadership, contributing to a culture of continuous learning.

- **Recognizing Your Leadership Weaknesses through story**

Emma, the head of a creative agency, was a whirlwind of artistic vision and innovation, consistently pushing her team to new heights of creativity. However, despite her prowess in the creative domain, Emma found herself out of her depth when it came to the financial aspects of her role. Budgeting, forecasting, and financial planning were areas that she had long avoided, a tendency that had once precipitated a severe cash flow crisis, nearly jeopardizing the agency's operations.

Realizing the risk her avoidance posed, not just to herself but to the entire agency, Emma decided it was time for a change. She recognized that to lead her agency effectively, she needed to confront her financial weaknesses head-on. With a resolve to turn this potential downfall into a stepping-stone for growth, Emma sought out a financial mentor—someone seasoned in the nuances of finance within the creative industry.

Under the guidance of her mentor, Emma began to demystify the financial elements that had once overwhelmed her. She also enrolled in a finance management workshop, committing herself to learn the very skills she had once shied away from. This dual approach—practical, hands-on learning complemented by expert mentoring—proved to be transformative.

As Emma's understanding deepened, so did her confidence. She started to integrate financial planning into her daily responsibilities, approaching budget meetings with the same creativity she brought to her design work. This newfound competence allowed her to not only manage her agency's finances more effectively but also to make strategic decisions that spurred growth and stability.

Emma's willingness to address and improve her financial acumen reshaped her leadership style, turning a previous weakness into a testament to her dedication to personal and professional development. Her journey inspired her team, proving that vulnerabilities can be transformed into strengths with courage and commitment. Under her more comprehensive leadership, the agency not only recovered from its previous setbacks but also moved forward with a stronger, more sustainable foundation.

5. The Importance of Self-Awareness in Leadership

Self-awareness is foundational in effective leadership. It helps you understand your impact on others, recognize areas for personal growth, and navigate challenges with composure. This awareness is critical for building strong relationships, making informed decisions, and fostering an authentic leadership style.

- **The Importance of Self-Awareness in Leadership through story**

Tom, a team leader in software development, was known for his technical expertise and innovative thinking. However, he had one issue that affected his leadership:

his mood swings. Tom's emotional ups and downs were becoming increasingly noticeable at work, impacting his team's morale and productivity. On his good days, the team felt motivated and inspired, but when Tom was in a bad mood, a cloud of negativity hung over the office.

Recognizing this pattern, Tom took a step back to reflect on the influence his moods had on his team. He realized that to lead effectively, he needed to provide a stable and positive environment. Determined to change, Tom began to work on managing his emotions more carefully, especially in the workplace.

He started practicing mindfulness and stress management techniques, such as meditation and regular exercise, to help regulate his emotional state. Tom also sought feedback from his team and mentors, which helped him become more aware of how his behavior affected others. This feedback was crucial in guiding his efforts to improve.

As Tom became more consistent in his interactions, his team responded positively. The atmosphere at work became lighter and more collaborative. Team members felt more comfortable and supported, leading to increased creativity and productivity. They knew what to expect from Tom, which made them feel more secure and confident in their roles.

This shift in Tom's approach to managing his emotions significantly enhanced his effectiveness as a leader. Not only did team dynamics improve, but Tom also developed stronger relationships with his colleagues. By becoming more emotionally stable, Tom fostered a positive and productive work environment that benefitted everyone involved.

Conclusion

The journey to understanding your strengths and weaknesses as a leader is ongoing and dynamic. It requires constant reflection, openness to feedback, and a commitment to self-improvement. By embracing both your strengths and your weaknesses, you can lead more effectively and inspire those around you to also strive for personal and professional growth.

As these stories illustrate, understanding your strengths and weaknesses is not just about introspection—it's about transformation. It's a dynamic process that involves feedback, reflection, and growth. Leaders like Alex, Sarah, Michael, Lisa, James, Emma, and Tom show us that by embracing both strengths and vulnerabilities, you can guide your team more effectively and inspire everyone around you to grow alongside you. In the end, effective leadership is about continuous self-improvement, crafted through the stories of our experiences and lessons learned.

Chapter 3

Step 2: Mastering the Art of Communication

Mastering the art of communication is essential in both personal and professional realms. Effective communication streamlines the transmission of thoughts, ideas, and information, making every interaction more meaningful and impactful. This chapter explores the nuances of crafting clear, impactful messages and the transformative power of empathetic listening.

1. The Power of Empathy in Communication

Empathy is the cornerstone of effective communication. It goes beyond simple understanding to a profound connection, where you truly grasp the emotions and perspectives of others. This connection does more than facilitate smoother conversations; it builds trust and fosters genuine relationships. By empathizing, you can engage in dialogues that not only reach their informational goals but also strengthen interpersonal bonds, leading to collaborative success in both personal and professional settings.

The Power of Empathy in Communication: Laura's Transformation

Laura was a project manager overseeing a team tasked with launching a new software product. The stakes were high, and the atmosphere among team members was tense, filled with frequent misunderstandings and disagreements. Laura noticed that meetings often ended with members feeling frustrated and unheard. Determined to change this dynamic, Laura decided to prioritize empathy in her communication approach.

She began by organizing one-on-one sessions with each team member, aiming to understand their personal and professional challenges deeply. During these sessions, Laura practiced active listening, nodding affirmatively and reflecting back what was said to ensure understanding. She asked open-ended questions to delve deeper into their concerns, making each team member feel valued and respected.

Over the following weeks, Laura's approach began to transform the team. Meetings became more collaborative and less confrontational. Team members started to open up, sharing ideas and solutions freely, knowing their viewpoints were appreciated. This newfound harmony led to innovative solutions for the software project, which was successfully launched ahead of schedule. The team's productivity soared, and they were recognized within the company for their exceptional teamwork. Laura's commitment to empathetic communication had not only resolved the team's issues but had also fostered a supportive and productive work environment.

Tailoring Your Message

A key hallmark of a skilled communicator is the ability to adjust their message based on the audience. This skill is crucial whether addressing a conference room or a coffee table chat. Understanding the cultural, emotional, and intellectual framework of your audience allows you to craft messages that resonate deeply, ensuring your words are not just heard but felt. This adaptive communication fosters a more engaging and responsive dialogue, enhancing the effectiveness of the interaction.

Tailoring Your Message: Mark's Cultural Adaptation

Mark, a seasoned sales director, was excited about the opportunity to expand his company's reach into Asia. He had a critical negotiation lined up with a potential

Japanese client, which could open doors to a significant market. However, during the initial meeting, he noticed his usual direct and assertive communication style was not resonating with the client, who seemed reserved and slightly uncomfortable.

Realizing the need for a change in approach, Mark quickly adapted. He switched to a more formal and respectful tone, honoring the client's cultural preference for humility and indirectness. He began using phrases like "We are honored to have the opportunity" and "We respectfully suggest," which aligned more closely with Japanese business etiquette.

This shift in communication style made a profound difference. The client warmed up to Mark, and the conversation flowed more smoothly. By the end of the meeting, they had agreed in principle to a deal, much to Mark's delight. This experience underscored the importance of cultural sensitivity in communication and taught Mark a valuable lesson in international business dealings.

Non-Verbal Communication and Feedback

The subtleties of communication extend far beyond the spoken word. Non-verbal cues—such as body language, facial expressions, and tone—play a critical role in how your message is perceived. An open posture or a warm tone can convey honesty and trustworthiness, while a furrowed brow or a sharp tone might signal frustration or disapproval. Master communicators are not only aware of their own non-verbal signals but also adept at reading others', allowing for a more nuanced exchange of ideas.

Non-Verbal Communication and Feedback: Anna's Therapeutic Breakthrough

Anna, a seasoned therapist, had a new client, Emily, who seemed perpetually tense and guarded during their sessions. Emily's arms were often crossed, and her responses were short, signaling discomfort. Anna knew she needed to create a more welcoming atmosphere to help Emily open up.

In the next session, Anna made a conscious effort to adjust her own non-verbal cues. She maintained a relaxed posture, kept her arms open, and often smiled gently to appear more approachable. She also mirrored Emily's body language subtly, leaning in slightly when Emily did, showing attentiveness.

These subtle changes helped Emily feel safer and more relaxed. Over time, she began to share more about her struggles, and her body language became more open and relaxed. This breakthrough was crucial in her therapy process, enabling deeper discussions and more effective treatment. Anna's thoughtful adjustment to her non-verbal communication had fostered a transformative therapeutic environment.

The Digital Age and Communication

With the digital revolution, the landscape of communication has expanded exponentially. Today's communicators must navigate a myriad of platforms, from emails and blogs to tweets and video calls. Each medium has its nuances and requires a specific tone and style. Effective digital communication demands clarity, brevity, and a keen sense of the recipient's perspective to avoid misinterpretations caused by the lack of physical cues. Embracing these new forms of communication with an adaptive mindset can broaden your influence and effectiveness across platforms.

The Digital Age and Communication: Sarah's Remote Leadership

Sarah, a marketing manager, faced significant challenges in keeping her remote team aligned and motivated. The shift to remote work had diluted the casual, collaborative spirit of her in-office team. Determined to regain this camaraderie, Sarah revamped her digital communication strategy.

She started sending out weekly video messages, where she spoke about team achievements and highlighted individual contributions. Her emails were concise and clear but included emoticons to add warmth and personality. She also initiated virtual coffee breaks where team members could catch up informally, just as they used to in the office kitchen.

These efforts paid off. The team felt more connected not only to the project but also to each other. Morale improved, and productivity followed suit. Sarah's adept use of digital tools to foster communication proved essential in maintaining team cohesion and motivation in a remote work environment.

Continuous Improvement

The journey to becoming an exceptional communicator is ongoing. The landscape of interaction is constantly shifting, demanding adaptability and continuous learning. Embracing this perpetual state of development is crucial for anyone looking to lead or influence effectively. Regularly engaging in communication skills training, seeking diverse perspectives, and applying new communication techniques to daily interactions can propel you towards greater proficiency and confidence.

Continuous Improvement: Tom's Pitch Perfection

Tom, an ambitious entrepreneur, was initially disheartened by the lukewarm response his business pitches received. Aware that effective communication was crucial, he committed to mastering this skill. He attended workshops where he learned the nuances of persuasive speaking and sought feedback from every presentation he gave.

Armed with new techniques and insights, Tom practiced relentlessly. He recorded his pitches, analyzed them, and refined his delivery, focusing on clarity and engagement. He learned to use stories and data effectively, making his presentations not only informative but also compelling.

Six months later, Tom's efforts bore fruit. He delivered a pitch for his startup that was met with enthusiasm and substantial financial backing. This success was a testament to his dedication to continuous improvement in communication. Tom's journey from novice to master communicator had equipped him with the skills to convey his vision compellingly and persuasively.

Key Takeaways for Leaders

For leaders, communication is not just a tool but also a core competency that can define their success. Effective leadership communication involves:

- **Active Listening:** Engage with what is being said, and show that you value others' contributions. This builds a culture of respect and openness.

- **Clarity and Precision:** Articulate your thoughts and instructions clearly to avoid misunderstandings.

- **Empathy:** Understanding your team's emotions and viewpoints can revolutionize your leadership approach, leading to higher morale and better team dynamics.

Story: Elena's Leadership Transformation

Elena, the CEO of a burgeoning tech startup, faced a critical juncture. Her company, rich in talent and innovation, was underperforming. Product launches were delayed, and team morale was noticeably low. The disconnect between the potential she saw and the outcomes being produced was frustrating. Recognizing that a fundamental change was necessary, Elena decided to delve deeper into the issues by engaging directly with her team at every level.

Initiating the Listening Tour

Elena launched what she called a "listening tour," a series of structured, in-depth conversations with employees across all departments—from software engineers to sales personnel. She dedicated entire days to these sessions, eschewing her usual responsibilities to ensure full focus and presence. Each meeting was carefully planned to foster an atmosphere of trust and openness. Elena encouraged her employees to share candidly, promising transparency and, more importantly, action based on their feedback.

Through these discussions, Elena uncovered a series of communication breakdowns that were at the heart of many of the company's issues. Many employees felt isolated within their roles, unaware of how their work impacted broader company objectives. Others expressed frustration over unclear project directions and perceived a lack of recognition for their contributions.

Strategic Changes and Implementation

Armed with these insights, Elena took decisive action. She overhauled the company's internal communication framework to ensure clarity and continuous feedback at all levels:

1. ***Regular Cross-Departmental Meetings***: *Elena introduced bi-weekly cross-departmental meetings where teams could present their progress and challenges. These meetings not only improved project transparency but also fostered a sense of unity and shared purpose across the company.*

2. ***Real-Time Digital Dashboard***: *To maintain transparency, a real-time digital dashboard was launched. This tool allowed everyone in the company to see how individual projects were advancing and how these contributed to the company's strategic goals. It became a vital tool for aligning efforts and celebrating collective achievements.*

3. ***Leadership Accessibility***: *Implementing an open-door policy, Elena made herself more available to her team, setting aside hours each week specifically reserved for employees to come in and discuss anything from project ideas to personal development. This policy extended to all senior managers, embedding a culture of accessibility and responsiveness throughout the leadership team.*

4. ***Communication Workshops***: *Understanding that effective communication needed to be a core competency at all levels, Elena sponsored workshops focusing on developing empathy, enhancing listening skills, and improving clarity in conveying complex information. These workshops were not just for managers but were made available to everyone within the organization.*

Transformative Outcomes

The changes Elena implemented had a transformative effect on the company. The atmosphere shifted from one of uncertainty and frustration to one of engagement and enthusiasm. Teams became more collaborative and proactive, with members feeling empowered to take initiative and voice their ideas.

Innovation flourished under the new system. A project that had been languishing in development for months was rapidly pushed to completion, leading to a breakthrough product that captured market attention and opened new revenue streams. Employee satisfaction scores soared, and turnover rates dropped, as staff felt more connected and valued than ever before.

Lasting Impact

Elena's commitment to transforming communication within her startup catalyzed its growth and helped it become a leading player in the tech industry. The company not only achieved and surpassed its performance goals but also cultivated a workplace environment that attracted top talent from across the globe. Elena's listening tour became a legendary part of the company's history, a testament to the power of leadership that listens and adapts. Her story exemplified how strategic changes in communication can create a lasting impact, driving a company to new heights of success and innovation.

Conclusion

The mastery of communication skills is essential for anyone looking to make a significant impact—whether in their personal lives or professional spheres. By continually refining these skills, you ensure that your ability to influence, motivate, and connect does not stagnate but grows stronger with time. Mastering the art of communication is not merely a skill, but a gateway to profound human connections and leadership success. When you refine your ability to express thoughts clearly, listen deeply, and resonate emotionally with others, you don't just communicate—you inspire, you understand, and you forge bonds that can withstand the tests of both time and challenge.

Core Strategies for Elevating Your Communication Skills:

1. **Pursue Continuous Learning**: Just as a sculptor shapes a masterpiece, so you too must craft your communication skills with precision and care. Engage in workshops, seek feedback, and challenge yourself in new speaking arenas. Each word spoken and heard is an opportunity to refine your art.

2. **Harness Emotional Intelligence**: Delve into the realm of emotions to truly connect with your audience. By tuning into your own feelings and those of others, you transform exchanges from mere transactions to meaningful interactions. This emotional alignment is the heart of impactful communication.

3. **Cultivate Active Listening**: Active listening is the secret melody behind every great conversation. It's about tuning into the underlying harmonies of dialogue, not just the surface lyrics. When you listen with intent, people feel seen and heard, and true understanding can flourish.

4. **Adapt and Personalize Your Approach**: Communication is not one-size-fits-all. Adjust your style to fit the contours of your audience, whether it is a boardroom of executives or a small team meeting. Adapting your message to the context and audience ensures it lands with the intended impact.

5. **Prioritize Clarity and Brevity**: In a world cluttered with information, clarity cuts through the noise. Be concise yet powerful in your communication. Every word should serve a purpose, either to build a bridge or to clear a path forward.

As you embark on this journey to master your communication skills, remember that every conversation is a step towards becoming a more effective leader and a more empathetic human. Your words have the power to change minds, open hearts, and inspire action.

Begin Today: Do not wait for the perfect moment to start improving your communication. The perfect moment is now. Every interaction today is an opportunity to practice, to improve, and to move closer to the communicator—and the leader—you aspire to be.

This journey of enhancing your communication skills is rich with rewards. It will open doors to new opportunities, deepen your relationships, and elevate your personal and professional life. Start today, and embrace the transformative power of effective communication. Remember, the path to leadership excellence is paved with the words you choose and the connections they forge. Let your communication be your legacy.

Chapter 4

Step 3: Developing Strategies to effectively Manage Change & Conflict

Change and conflict are integral to any dynamic organization. Understanding how to manage these elements can transform potential disruptions into opportunities for growth and innovation. This chapter focuses on strategies that leaders can employ to navigate organizational changes and resolve conflicts effectively, ensuring long-term success.

Clear Communication: A Foundation for Success

Effective communication is essential in managing organizational change. It involves more than just sharing information; it is about making sure everyone understands and accepts what is happening. When changes are on the horizon, explaining their purpose, expected outcomes, and potential impacts on each team can lessen uncertainty and anxiety. Regular team meetings, detailed email updates, and open Q&A sessions are all effective methods for maintaining transparency. By thoroughly explaining the reasons behind changes, leaders can align their teams with the organization's vision and minimize resistance.

Enhanced Methods for Effective Communication:

- **Regular Team Meetings:** These should not just be informative but interactive, encouraging questions and discussions to ensure clarity.

- **Detailed Email Updates:** Emails can provide comprehensive information and be a good reference for employees to understand the timelines and expectations during transitions.

- **Open Q&A Sessions:** These sessions offer a safe space for employees to voice concerns and get immediate responses, which helps in mitigating rumors and misinformation.

By thoroughly explaining the reasons behind changes and discussing how these alterations align with the organization's broader goals, leaders can foster a sense of understanding and reduce resistance. This approach not only keeps everyone on the same page but also strengthens the collective resolve to move forward together.

Clear Communication: Story of Transformation

Janet's Journey with the New System

Janet, a seasoned department head at a regional healthcare provider, faced her biggest challenge yet: implementing an entirely new electronic health records system. The initial announcement met with considerable resistance. Staff were anxious about the change, worried about the learning curve and potential disruptions to patient care. Recognizing the need for clear and compassionate communication, Janet organized a series of town hall meetings, each tailored to different teams and their specific concerns.

At these meetings, Janet didn't just present; she connected. She shared her own apprehensions about the new system and her confidence in the team's ability to overcome challenges together. She patiently answered every question, ensuring no one felt ignored. Her transparent approach and the assurance that no one would face this change alone turned skepticism into a shared commitment. Over time, the team not only adapted to but also championed the new system, praising its efficiency and the improvements in patient care. Janet's commitment to clear, empathetic communication transformed potential upheaval into a triumph for the organization.

Inclusive Participation: Empowering Your Team

Inclusive participation is about more than informing team members of changes; it involves actively seeking their input and incorporating their feedback into both planning and execution. This approach not only improves the quality of change initiatives through diverse perspectives but also fosters a sense of ownership among employees. Techniques like brainstorming sessions, workshops, and focus groups allow employees to express their concerns and suggestions, making them feel valued and respected. This collaborative method not only reduces resistance but also leverages the collective intelligence of the workforce to enhance and fine-tune the change process.

Strategies for Fostering Inclusive Participation:

- **Brainstorming Sessions:** These sessions allow employees to contribute ideas and express concerns, making them feel valued and considered.

- **Workshops and Focus Groups:** These settings provide structured opportunities for deeper exploration of specific changes, where employees can test new systems or processes and give feedback based on their hands-on experiences.

- **Feedback Mechanisms:** Ensuring there are easy ways for staff to offer their insights at any point in the change process helps leaders collect and consider a wide range of viewpoints.

This collaborative approach not only smooths the path for change by reducing resistance but also taps into the collective intelligence of the workforce, refining and optimizing the process based on a variety of insights.

Inclusive Participation

Story of Engagement: Carlos and the Shift to Automation

Carlos led a manufacturing firm grappling with the transition to automation—a move essential for competitiveness yet fraught with employee apprehension. Understanding the importance of inclusive participation, Carlos set up innovation labs where employees could interact firsthand with the new machinery under the guidance of experts. These weren't just demonstrations; they were interactive sessions where workers could voice concerns, suggest modifications, and understand the technology's impact on their roles.

Carlos took this feedback seriously, adjusting protocols to better fit the team's expertise and comfort levels. The workshops became a core part of the transition strategy, transforming fear into fascination and resistance into engagement. By the time the automation was fully implemented, the employees were not just proficient; they were enthusiastic proponents of the technology. Carlos's dedication to making everyone a part of the change process cultivated a deep sense of ownership across the workforce, culminating in a smoother than expected transition and enhanced production lines.

Support and Resources: Equipping for Change

Providing necessary support and resources is crucial for helping employees navigate change. This includes training programs tailored to new skills and knowledge, as well as ongoing access to support materials like manuals, FAQs, and help desks. Coaching and mentoring are equally important; they offer personalized support and help individuals tackle specific challenges related to change. For instance, a mentorship program can connect less experienced employees with seasoned veterans who guide them through transitions, providing advice and encouragement that significantly ease the adaptation process.

Key Elements of Support and Resources:

- **Tailored Training Programs:** Specific training sessions designed to address the skills gaps that new tools or processes might introduce.

- **Continuous Access to Support Materials:** Ongoing availability of manuals, FAQs, and help desks to assist employees as they navigate new systems or procedures.

- **Coaching and Mentoring:** Personalized support through mentoring programs can help individuals more effectively manage the personal and professional challenges posed by change.

For example, initiating a mentorship program that pairs less experienced employees with seasoned veterans can facilitate smoother transitions by providing continuous guidance, reassurance, and support.

Support and Resources:

Story of Empowerment: Leah's Training Initiative

Leah, a creative director at an up-and-coming advertising agency, noticed a significant dip in efficiency as her team struggled with the transition to advanced digital reporting tools. Determined to turn this around, Leah organized a comprehensive support system. She initiated weekly training workshops led by digital experts and provided team members with continuous access to learning resources like tutorial videos, step-by-step guides, and a dedicated help desk.

Each session was designed to build confidence and mastery over the new tools. Leah's approach went beyond technical training; she fostered an environment where mistakes were seen as learning opportunities. Gradually, the team's confidence grew, and they began to leverage the new tools to extract deeper insights into consumer behavior, significantly boosting the agency's capabilities in data-driven marketing. Leah's foresight and commitment to empowering her team with the right tools and knowledge ushered in a new era of creativity and effectiveness.

Positive Work Environment: Cultivating Collaboration and Teamwork

A positive work environment that promotes collaboration and teamwork can greatly enhance the effectiveness of change management. Leaders should foster a culture where teamwork is celebrated and collaborative efforts are acknowledged. Team-building exercises and joint problem-solving tasks can strengthen mutual trust and cooperation. Additionally, recognizing and celebrating team achievements during times of change can lift morale and motivate employees to collectively tackle new challenges.

Approaches to Cultivate a Positive Work Environment:

- **Team-Building Exercises:** Activities designed to strengthen relationships and improve teamwork can be vital in times of change.

- **Recognition and Rewards:** Acknowledging and celebrating team efforts and achievements helps maintain morale and motivation during transitions.

Such strategies encourage collaboration and help forge strong bonds among team members, which are crucial for navigating the upheavals of change successfully.

Positive Work Environment

Story of Unity: Tom's Team-Building Triumphs

Tom faced the daunting task of merging two software development teams with a history of rivalry. To forge unity, Tom introduced monthly team-building retreats focused on activities that required collaboration and problem-solving. He also implemented "celebration Fridays" where teams gathered to acknowledge weekly achievements, share learning points, and discuss project updates in a casual setting.

These initiatives broke down barriers, allowing team members to see each other's strengths and foster mutual respect. The retreats became events that everyone looked forward to, and the Fridays helped maintain a spirit of camaraderie and transparency. This shift in team dynamics led to innovative software solutions that pushed the company to the forefront of technology startups. Tom's efforts to create a supportive and collaborative environment turned a fragmented group into the company's strongest asset.

Structured Change Management Plans: Roadmaps to Success

Creating a structured change management plan involves outlining clear steps, defining roles and responsibilities, and setting realistic timelines for each phase. This roadmap should be transparent and accessible to all employees, with regular updates to reflect adjustments or new insights gained during implementation. Effective plans also include mechanisms for monitoring progress and measuring outcomes, helping maintain accountability and adapt strategies as needed to achieve goals.

Components of an Effective Change Management Plan:

- **Clear Steps and Defined Roles:** Everyone should know what to expect and what is expected of them.

- **Regular Updates:** Keeping the plan current and reflective of any shifts in strategy or objectives is crucial for maintaining alignment and momentum.

- **Monitoring and Measuring Outcomes:** Regularly assessing progress and outcomes ensures the plan stays on track and adjustments are made as necessary.

Structured Change Management Plans:

Story of Strategic Success: Samantha's Seamless Integration

Samantha, tasked with the integration of a newly acquired solar technology company, faced a tight timeline and high stakes. She crafted a detailed integration plan, clearly outlining every phase, assigning roles, and setting checkpoints. She held weekly briefings to update everyone on progress and gather input, making adjustments in real-time to address emerging challenges.

Her meticulous planning and inclusive approach minimized disruptions and quickly aligned the new teams with the company's vision. Samantha's strategic foresight ensured not just a successful integration but also spurred rapid growth in the company's solar division, setting new standards in the industry for efficient and effective mergers. Her ability to manage complex changes with precision and inclusivity turned a high-risk move into a resounding success.

Example of Effective Change Management

Embracing Change: A Case Study on Effective Change Management in a Technology Firm

Imagine you are at the helm of a technology company, ready to roll out a brand-new system that promises to revolutionize how your team works. However, there is a challenge: your team is clinging to the old ways, wary of the new changes. How do you guide your crew through these turbulent waters to embrace a new direction?

A technology firm found itself grappling with significant upheaval as it embarked on transitioning to a new customer relationship management (CRM) system. The initial shift was fraught with challenges, rooted primarily in insufficient preparation and palpable resistance from employees who were accustomed to the old system.

The leadership at the firm knew that introducing a new customer relationship management (CRM) system was not just about new software; it was about helping people adapt. Here is how they successfully navigated this change.

Recognizing the crucial need for a more structured approach to manage this critical change effectively, the leadership team formulated a comprehensive change management plan.

Strategic Approach to Change Management:

Tailored Training Sessions: Just as a captain adjusts the sails to suit the winds, the firm customized training programs to align with the diverse roles across the company. Understanding that the cornerstone of successful adoption lies in adept user competence, the firm rolled out a series of training sessions meticulously tailored to various roles within the organization. These sessions were designed not just to introduce the new system, but also to address specific operational needs across different departments, ensuring that each team member could navigate the new system with confidence.

Regular Progress Updates: With the precision of a seasoned navigator, the leadership regularly charted their progress, sharing these updates with the entire crew. To foster an environment of transparency and trust, the firm committed to providing regular updates on the transition's progress. This continuous flow of information helped mitigate fears and built a shared understanding of how the transition was unfolding, what milestones had been achieved, and what steps lay ahead.

Forums for Feedback: Recognizing that a successful voyage depends on the input of every crew member, the company established forums for open dialogue. Acknowledging that successful change must involve input from those affected by it, the company established forums where employees could freely voice their concerns and offer feedback. These platforms not only served to gather invaluable insights from users but also empowered employees, making them feel valued and involved in the change process.

Change Champions: To bridge the gap between the old and the new, **'change champions'** were appointed from various departments. To enhance communication between management and staff and to facilitate smoother information flow, the firm designated **'change champions'** from different departments. These individuals acted as liaisons, communicating employee feedback to management and disseminating strategic decisions back to their teams. Their role was pivotal in ensuring that communication remained effective and responsive across all levels of the organization.

Outcome of the Change Management Initiative:

The firm's strategic initiatives fostered a new culture of adaptability and openness, leading to a successful integration of the new CRM system. The strategic change management efforts culminated in a significant shift in employee attitudes towards the new CRM system. Initial resistance gave way to acceptance, and skepticism was replaced by active participation. The tailored training sessions equipped the employees with the necessary skills and confidence to navigate the new system effectively, while the regular updates and feedback mechanisms ensured that they felt supported throughout the transition process. The role of change champions proved invaluable in ensuring that communication remained fluid and constructive.

Reflecting on the Journey:

This narrative illustrates not just the importance of effective change management strategies but also the profound impact they can have on a company's internal dynamics and overall success. The emotional and practical transformations experienced by the teams highlight a pivotal truth: navigating change effectively requires a blend of strategic foresight and deep empathy.

This case study exemplifies the profound impact of thoughtful and well-executed change management strategies. The firm's approach not only facilitated the technical integration of the new CRM system but also fostered a positive and inclusive culture that embraced the change. The leadership's commitment to detailed preparation, open communication, and employee engagement transformed a challenging transition into a resounding success story, underscoring the critical role of adaptive and empathetic leadership in times of change.

Through this narrative, it becomes evident that managing technological change is much more about understanding and guiding people through the transition than it is about the technology itself. The emotional and practical journeys undertaken by teams and leaders highlight how challenges can be transformed into opportunities for growth and innovation, ultimately enhancing organizational resilience and capability.

As we draw this discussion to a close, consider how you can apply these insights to your own leadership challenges. Whether you are steering a team through minor adjustments or transformative changes, remember that the success of your voyage hinges not just on the route you take, but also on how you lead your crew through the journey.

Take Action:

Are you ready to lead your team through change? Start by assessing your current strategies and consider how integrating tailored training, regular updates, feedback mechanisms, and dedicated change advocates might enhance your approach. Every step you take in refining your change management strategies not only prepares your team for upcoming transitions but also strengthens the resilience and agility of your organization. Let your team join you on this voyage of discovery and transformation, and let them set sail together towards a future marked by innovation and success.

Your Turn to Steer:
Are you ready to lead your team through changes? Start by looking at your own strategies. Could you improve how you train, inform, or involve your team? Even small adjustments in how you manage change can make a big difference in getting your team onboard and ready for new challenges.

Remember, it is not just about the destination but how you get there together. So, set the course, prepare your crew, and lead your team toward new horizons with confidence and care.

Conclusion

Each story highlights the profound impact of strategically applied change management strategies. From Janet's commitment to clear communication to Samantha's meticulous planning, these narratives showcase how different elements of change management can come together to create successful transformations in any organization. By following these examples, leaders can inspire their teams and guide their organizations through change, not just surviving but also thriving in new circumstances.

Navigating organizational change and managing conflict demand a comprehensive strategy that taps into several key areas: clear communication, inclusive participation, ample support, a nurturing work environment, and a robust change management plan. By skillfully deploying these strategies, leaders can guarantee that their organizations do not just weather the storms of change but also flourish, coming out stronger and more cohesive.

Key Strategies for Navigating Organizational Change

1. **Clear Communication:** The cornerstone of any successful change initiative is crystal-clear communication. Clear, transparent communication forms the backbone of successful change management. It ensures that every team member understands the what, why, and how of the change process. This clarity reduces misunderstandings and aligns the team towards common goals.

2. **Inclusive Participation:** Engaging all stakeholders in the planning and execution phases of change fosters a sense of ownership and acceptance. When employees are part of the conversation and decision-making process, they are more likely to support and champion the change.

3. **Sufficient Support:** Providing adequate resources and support during times of change is crucial. This might include training programs to upskill employees, access to new tools and technologies, or emotional and psychological support to help staff navigate the transition.

4. **Positive Work Environment:** Cultivating a positive atmosphere that promotes well-being and job satisfaction can alleviate the stress associated with change. Leaders should strive to maintain morale by recognizing efforts, celebrating milestones, and encouraging a balance between work and personal life.

5. **Structured Change Management Plan:** A well-defined change management plan acts as a roadmap, guiding the entire process. This plan should outline the steps of the change, anticipated challenges, mitigation strategies, and metrics for success, ensuring that the organization remains on track and adaptive.

By integrating these strategies, leaders can transform their organizations into entities that view change not as a hurdle but as a springboard for innovation and growth. Each strategy contributes uniquely to managing change, creating a culture that not only adapts to new realities but also thrives on them. Leaders who embrace these practices ensure their organizations are resilient, agile, and equipped to meet future challenges head-on.

Chapter 5

Step 4: Building Relationships with Team Members & Stakeholders

Introduction

Building relationships with team members and stakeholders is not merely a requirement of leadership—it is the very essence of it. The most effective leaders grasp the transformative power of genuine connections. These relationships foster a thriving work environment and catalyze the collective success of the organization.

Imagine leadership as the art of weaving a vast tapestry of relationships, each thread vibrant with potential and every connection critical to the stunning final image. Effective leaders understand that forging deep, meaningful connections with both team members and stakeholders is crucial, not just for a thriving work environment but for the very success of the organization itself. This chapter delves into the heart of relationship-building, exploring key strategies and real-life examples to illuminate the path for emerging leaders.

Building Effective Team Relationships as a Leader

Imagine you are a conductor of an orchestra. Each musician plays a unique instrument, essential for the harmony of the whole. Similarly, as a leader, understanding the individual strengths and weaknesses of each team member is crucial. It involves more than just managing them; it's about encouraging a symphony of collaboration.

The foundation of effective team management lies in forging strong, supportive relationships with each member. This requires a leader to practice open and honest communication, actively listen, and show genuine care and interest in the well-being of team members.

Understanding each member's strengths and weaknesses allows leaders to offer personalized support, thereby fostering an environment where everyone can thrive and contribute optimally.

Passionate leadership in developing these relationships is key. It involves more than just professional interactions; it requires a commitment to creating a team dynamic that values trust, respect, and mutual support. Leaders should work to resolve conflicts constructively and provide opportunities for team bonding, which strengthens trust and cooperation among team members.

Case in Point: Emma's Approach

Consider Emma, a project manager with a keen eye for detail and a deeper understanding of human dynamics. Emma's approach to leadership is profoundly relational. As a project manager overseeing a diverse team, she likens her role to that of a gardener nurturing a variety of plants. Each team member, like a different species in a garden, requires unique care—some thrive on public recognition, while others blossom under the gentle sun of private encouragement. Under her leadership, a once underperforming team blossomed into a powerhouse of productivity and innovation.

Deep Dive into Emma's Strategy:

Emma instituted a monthly "Growth Chat" initiative, scheduling individual meetings with each team member to discuss not just current projects but their long-term career aspirations and personal well-being.

These discussions, held in the comforting ambience of the office's sunlit lounge, allow her to connect on a deeper level, making each team member feel uniquely valued. This personalized approach not only boosts morale but also aligns individual goals with the team's objectives, creating a unified, motivated workforce.

Emma's personalized approach has transformed her team from a group of individually talented professionals into a cohesive unit pulsating with collaborative energy and innovative output.

Emma, as a project manager and leader, exemplifies this. Recognizing the diverse capabilities of her team, she tailors her interactions and support to fit each member's needs, fostering a culture where everyone feels valued and understood. Her team's cohesion and productivity are testaments to the effectiveness of her personalized approach.

Strategies for Building Relationships with Team Members

1. **Open and Honest Communication**: Lisa, who leads a dynamic marketing team, is a paragon of transparency. Her monthly town hall meetings are legendary within the company—known for their spirited discussions and heartfelt exchanges. Here, beneath the soft glow of eco-friendly lights in the spacious conference hall, team members freely voice concerns, celebrate milestones, and brainstorm solutions.

Leaders like Lisa ensure that transparency is the cornerstone of their leadership style. By sharing not only successes but also challenges, they create a culture of trust and openness.

2. **Active Listening**: Tom's leadership transformation began with his commitment to enhance his listening skills. Every Wednesday, he holds office hours exclusively reserved for team consultations. These sessions, taking place in his warmly decorated office filled with plants and art, are not just about business but are a testament to his genuine interest in their professional and personal narratives.

Tom, a team leader, dedicates part of his weekly schedule to one-on-one sessions with his team members, not to instruct but to listen. This simple practice has led to improved morale and innovative ideas.

3. **Empowering Team Members**: By delegating meaningful responsibilities and providing the necessary tools and support, leaders empower their team members to take initiative and drive their own professional growth.

Alex introduced the innovative 'Project Lead' program, where team members, regardless of rank, are given the helm of projects or meetings in rotation. This initiative, symbolically represented by a ceremonial 'Captain's Hat' passed among the team, has not only diversified leadership within the group but also invigorated the team with a sense of ownership and pride.

Cultivating Positive Relationships with Stakeholders

For leaders, stakeholders are not just external entities; they are integral contributors to the organization's narrative. Effective communication and trust-building with stakeholders like clients, investors, and partners are paramount.

Similarly, building relationships with stakeholders such as clients, investors, and partners is equally vital. These relationships should be characterized by transparency and constructive communication, which help in building trust and support for critical decisions and initiatives.

A leader's ability to establish and nurture these relationships can greatly influence the organization's reputation and long-term success.

Engaging stakeholders with a passionate approach involves recognizing their needs and concerns, ensuring that their voices are heard and valued. This not only enhances the relationship but also aligns the organization's objectives with stakeholder expectations, facilitating smoother cooperation and support.

A Strategic Shift: John's Initiative

John, a senior leader in a tech firm, understands that the vitality of his company hinges on the robustness of its external relationships. He champions a stakeholder-centric approach, recognizing that investors, partners, and clients are not mere contributors but integral to the narrative of his company's success.

John's Strategic Initiatives: Quarterly, John organizes the "Stakeholder Summit," an event that transforms the company's austere boardroom into a vibrant forum of ideas. Here, amidst informal setups and refreshments, stakeholders discuss the company's trajectory, brainstorm over new initiatives, and refine strategies. This collaborative atmosphere is punctuated with digital polls and live feedback mechanisms, ensuring that each voice is heard and valued, deepening their investment emotionally and financially in the company's future.

John, as a senior leader at a tech firm, knew that his company's growth depended significantly on how well he engaged with stakeholders. He made concerted efforts to keep them informed and involved in decision-making processes, which not only enhanced transparency but also solidified trust and support for strategic initiatives.

Cultivating Strong Stakeholder Connections

Building robust relationships with stakeholders involves recognizing and respecting their perspectives and needs. Successful leaders are proactive in their engagement, ensuring stakeholders feel valued and understood.

Effective Engagement: Mia's Roundtable Discussions

Mia, leading a non-profit organization, regularly organizes roundtable discussions with key stakeholders to discuss the organization's direction. She treats stakeholder engagement with the meticulous care of a curator arranging an art exhibit. Her roundtable discussions, often held in the community hall adorned with projects funded by the stakeholders themselves, serve as a testament to the organization's impact and a canvas for future ventures.

Mia's Roundtable Impact: Each session is meticulously planned to foster an atmosphere of inclusivity and collaboration. Stakeholders, surrounded by the tangible results of their contributions, engage in discussions that are less about oversight and more about visionary contributions to the community. Mia ensures that each voice is not only heard but also celebrated, weaving their insights into the fabric of the organization's strategy.

These sessions provide a platform for stakeholders to voice their opinions and feel genuinely involved in the organization's journey.

Enhancing Leadership through Relationship Building

True leadership transcends mere interaction. It involves deep emotional intelligence, the ability to resolve conflicts gracefully, and the cultivation of a diverse and inclusive work environment.

Empathy in Action: Alex's Leadership

Alex has developed a reputation for his empathetic leadership style. By genuinely understanding and addressing his team's concerns, he has not only resolved conflicts but also fostered a loyal and highly motivated team. Alex's approach to leadership beautifully exemplifies the transformative power of empathy. In a corporate world where deadlines and targets often overshadow personal interactions, Alex stands out by placing a strong emphasis on understanding and addressing the unique needs and concerns of each team member. This approach has not only dissolved potential conflicts but has also woven a fabric of deep trust and mutual respect within his team.

Imagine a typical Monday morning where tensions are high due to an upcoming project deadline. Instead of pushing his team harder, Alex calls a brief meeting. Here, he encourages his team members to voice any concerns and share personal hurdles that might impact their work. In these meetings, Alex listens — truly listens — to each voice, acknowledging their challenges and assuring them of his support.

For instance, when Sarah, a dedicated team member, expressed her struggle with balancing work and her responsibilities as a new parent, Alex didn't just note it; he acted. He adjusted her work hours and provided access to resources for managing her tasks more effectively. This not only helped Sarah manage her stress but also inspired her colleagues to speak up and trust in Alex's leadership. They saw firsthand that their leader valued their well-being as much as the company's goals.

Through his actions, Alex teaches a powerful lesson in leadership: that true leaders do not just lead; they listen and adapt to foster a supportive and productive environment. His team, motivated by his genuine concern and proactive support, works not out of obligation but out of loyalty and dedication. They know they are respected and valued beyond their output.

This kind of leadership creates a ripple effect. As team members feel supported, their job satisfaction and productivity soar, reducing turnover and building a resilient team that can face challenges head-on. Alex's story is a testament to the idea that when leaders nurture their teams with empathy and understanding, they build not just a more effective workforce but also a loyal and spirited community. This not only elevates the entire team's performance but also sets a standard of leadership that inspires others to follow, proving that the heart of effective leadership truly lies in empathy and genuine connection.

Strategies for Engaging Team Members and Stakeholders

1. **Recognition and Appreciation**: Celebrating individual and team successes publicly can significantly boost morale and promote a culture of achievement and appreciation.

2. **Providing Growth Opportunities**: Leaders who invest in the development of their team through training and career opportunities cultivate a more engaged and capable workforce.

3. **Consistent and Constructive Feedback**: Constructive feedback is crucial for professional development. Leaders like Sarah ensure it is delivered in a manner that is supportive and empowering, not critical.

Conclusion

Mastering the art of relationship-building transforms leaders into architects of harmony and catalysts for success within their organizations. By embracing the strategies illustrated in this chapter and embodying qualities of empathy, transparency, and genuine interest in the well-being of others, leaders forge lasting bonds that elevate both individual and collective success. Through vivid storytelling and strategic insights, this chapter inspires leaders to act with heart and purpose, guiding them to cultivate relationships that resonate with trust and mutual respect.

Building Bridges with Heart and Purpose

This chapter, through compelling narratives and insightful strategies, encourages leaders to engage deeply and meaningfully, to act with heart and purpose. It provides a blueprint for cultivating relationships that are rooted in trust and mutual respect—relationships that are not merely transactional but transformational.

Leaders who excel in relationship-building recognize that such connections are not automatic. They require a sustained commitment and a heartfelt interest in the lives and successes of team members and stakeholders alike. This commitment is what turns routine interactions into deep, impactful engagements.

The Continuous Journey of Relationship-Building

The art of building and sustaining impactful relationships demands ongoing effort and a sincere investment in the growth and welfare of others. Leaders who master this art not only propel their teams and organizations towards success but also make a lasting impression on everyone they interact with.

By integrating the strategies outlined in this chapter, you can significantly boost your effectiveness as a leader. You will foster a culture where mutual respect and cooperation are the norms, not the exceptions. These relationships, built on the foundations of empathy and transparency, will serve as the cornerstone of both personal and organizational achievement.

In essence, relationship-building is more than a skill—it is a leadership philosophy that, when practiced diligently, enriches both the leader and the broader community. Implement these lessons to not only enhance your leadership but also to create a legacy of positive, enduring impact.

Remember, the art of building and sustaining relationships requires continuous effort and genuine interest in the welfare of team members and stakeholders alike. Leaders who master this art not only drive their teams and organizations to success but also leave a lasting impact on everyone they interact with. By implementing the strategies outlined in this chapter, you can enhance your leadership effectiveness and foster a culture of mutual respect and cooperation.

༄

Conclusion

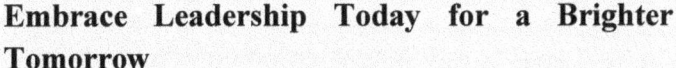

Embrace Leadership Today for a Brighter Tomorrow

Leadership is not just a skill—it is a transformational force that shapes every aspect of your personal and professional life. When you commit to enhancing your leadership abilities, you are not just improving your own prospects; you are elevating the experiences and opportunities of everyone around you.

Embark on Your Leadership Adventure

Start your journey by seizing every chance to lead, whether that is steering a project at work, volunteering in your community, or stepping up in social settings. These real-world experiences are the forge in which true leadership is tempered, giving you a robust platform to practice, refine, and perfect your skills.

Learn from the Masters

Seek out mentors whose footsteps echo the halls of success—leaders who have faced challenges with grace and determination. Their wisdom and insights can light your path, turning obstacles into stepping stones that lead to personal growth and achievement.

Cultivate a Growth Mindset

Leadership is a lifelong pursuit that thrives on curiosity and resilience. Embrace challenges as opportunities to grow, and never shy away from a chance to learn. This mindset will not only prepare you for the complexities of leadership but also inspire those you lead to adopt the same forward-thinking attitude.

Enhance Your Emotional Intelligence

Understanding and managing your emotions, and empathizing with others, are at the core of influential leadership. Develop your emotional intelligence to foster deeper relationships, build trust, and create a team dynamic that is supportive and strong.

Join the Learning Revolution

Dive into workshops, books, and seminars that focus on honing leadership skills. Each educational experience adds a layer to your understanding, equipping you with the tools needed to lead with confidence and insight.

Lead by Example

The most effective leaders are those who show, not just tell. By demonstrating integrity, dedication, and compassion, you set a standard for your team. This not only fosters a positive work environment but also encourages your team to reach their highest potential.

Foster Open Communication

Encourage a culture of transparency and open dialogue. When team members feel their voices are heard and valued, they're more engaged and invested in the mission. This openness not only strengthens the team but also enhances collective problem-solving and innovation.

Develop Potential in Others

True leaders recognize and nurture the potential in their teams. Challenge your team with new opportunities while providing the support they need to succeed. This not only promotes individual growth but also strengthens the team's overall capability and morale.

Steps to Enhance Your Leadership Skills:

Seek Leadership Opportunities:

Story of Clara's Initiative: Clara, a mid-level manager at a bustling technology firm, faced her biggest career challenge yet when she volunteered to lead a high-stakes, cross-departmental project aimed at overhauling the company's outdated communication systems. Initially, doubts crept in about her capability to handle such a significant task, especially given the diverse and occasionally conflicting personalities on her team. Determined, Clara used her deep understanding of company culture and individual team dynamics to foster a spirit of collaboration. Her leadership transformed a disjointed group into a cohesive unit that not only met but exceeded project goals. This triumph did not go unnoticed—her successful management of the project significantly boosted her reputation within the company, leading to her well-deserved promotion.

Pursue Mentorship:

Marcus's Mentorship Journey: When Marcus first stepped into his role as a nonprofit director, he felt overwhelmed by the expectations and the complexity of challenges he had to navigate. Recognizing the need for guidance, he sought out Elaine, a seasoned executive with over 30 years of experience in the nonprofit sector. Elaine's mentorship was transformative for Marcus, providing not just technical guidance but also teaching him the subtleties of nonprofit leadership, including stakeholder engagement, conflict resolution, and strategic planning. Their monthly coffee meetings became a cherished ritual for Marcus, offering him a safe space to voice concerns and learn from Elaine's rich trove of experiences. This relationship was pivotal in shaping Marcus into a confident leader, capable of steering his organization towards impactful community service and growth.

Engage in Continuous Learning:

Sophia's Leadership Workshops: Sophia, an aspiring entrepreneur with a vision to revolutionize the tech accessory market, understood early on that leadership would be crucial to her success. She immersed herself in leadership workshops and seminars, each session packed with insights into negotiation, team management, and market strategy. These were not just educational opportunities; they were networking goldmines that connected her with fellow entrepreneurs and potential investors. Her dedication to continuous learning helped her adapt her business model to better meet market demands, ultimately securing a substantial investment during a pitch to a panel of high-profile venture capitalists.

Foster Emotional Intelligence:

Elijah's Emotional Mastery: Leading a team in a high-stress financial trading firm, Elijah noticed a worrying trend of burnout and high turnover. He initiated "Wellness Wednesdays," where the team would start with a half-hour session focused on meditation and stress relief techniques before diving into their high-stakes trading day. Elijah actively participated, sharing his own experiences and strategies for managing stress. This initiative not only brought his team closer but also significantly enhanced their overall productivity and job satisfaction. The decrease in burnout rates and the positive feedback from the team were testaments to the power of emotional intelligence in leadership.

Adopt a Growth Mindset:

Nina's Approach to Failure: Nina led a software development team that recently experienced a significant setback with a failed project launch. Instead of finger pointing, Nina saw this as a crucial learning opportunity. She organized a series of "Learning From Failure" workshops where the team could openly discuss what went wrong and brainstorm improvements for future projects. These workshops helped dispel any lingering blame and turned the focus towards growth and innovation. Nina's ability to guide her team through adversity strengthened their resolve and cohesiveness, setting them up for future successes.

By committing to these actionable steps, you begin a transformative journey that not only advances your career but also enriches your personal life. Leadership is a continuous voyage of self-improvement and dedication. As you evolve, so does your ability to impact positively on the lives of others—inspiring them, guiding them, and helping them achieve their full potential.

Remember that Leadership is ultimately about making a difference. It is about leaving a mark on the world, however big or small, that speaks of your commitment to fostering growth, inspiring change, and leading by example. Start today—embrace your potential as a leader and watch as doors open not just for you, but also for all those you guide along the way. Remember, the journey of leadership is as rewarding as the destination.

Final Thoughts: Leadership as a Life-Changing Force

By investing in your leadership skills today, you set the stage for a future rich with opportunities—not just for yourself, but for everyone you influence. Leadership is more than a role; it is a commitment to rise above, to transform challenges into victories, and to guide others along the path of success.

Start this transformative journey today, and witness the profound impact vibrant leadership can have on the world around you. Embrace the challenge, and watch as your world transforms.

www.ingramcontent.com/pod-product-compliance
Lightning Source LLC
LaVergne TN
LVHW061558070526
838199LV00077B/7096